PRETTY TREES ON THE HILL

A Place I Go to Sit, It Is Pretty There

LARRY SELIG

iUniverse books may be ordered through booksellers or by contacting:

iUniverse
1663 Liberty Drive
Bloomington, IN 47403
www.iuniverse.com
844-349-9409

ISBN: 978-1-6632-4506-9 (sc)
ISBN: 978-1-6632-4507-6 (hc)
ISBN: 978-1-6632-4508-3 (e)

Library of Congress Control Number: 2022916520

Print information available on the last page.

iUniverse rev. date: 01/24/2023

CONTENTS

CHAPTER 1

Found a Spot in Kingston

February 15, 2020

My email address is seliglarry1@gmail.com. Let me know if you enjoy the book.

I've found a spot down here in Kingston, and it's a great spot. I like it, and I believe it helps me. I feel wonderful there. I drink coffee, and I sit and stay there for a while; you know, I'm always thinking.

There's a road that goes all the way to a river; I call it the creek. It's nice up there too. I like the creek and the woods, and seeing the pretty trees along the walk is so cool. I ride my bike right to the end, which is a ways away from my spot. Still, I walk it, when I'm not riding my bike. It's nice.

Well, I go to Kingston a lot. I ride everywhere in Kingston. The trails are good, and I ride my bike along them. I call Kingston a little town, but it's more a village. There are pretty stores, though, and places you can go to—including a superstore, which I like. I go there sometimes to get things.

A photo of my spot I took another way that I like on the first

CHAPTER 2

I Used to Live in Kingston

I used to live in Kingston. It's not far from where I live now, and I like going there. You never know; there may be a big thing there. Me, I get these ideas going through my brain. As for one I had recently, I asked the owners before I did more than I should. And when they gave me the OK to place a marker with the name of the spot I wanted to name, that's what I did. I took my hammer and nails, and off I went. I thought that was cool. The golf field is right up top of the hill, so they cautioned me to be careful of that—and not get hit with a golf ball (laugh out loud).

There are many places you can go in Kingston and pathways you can take to get them. There's a place where people go outside when weather is nice. They sing for the seniors or anyone who wants to come. I think that's great. A lot of my friends used to live in Kingston. Some have moved, though, and there aren't many of them left there for me to go see. But I have that spot. I will be going there.

I could turn Kingston into something. I always get in a lot of good thinking; I have a lot of things going through my mind. When I was younger, I thought of things, but I never did anything about it. Well, I never thought what I was thinking would go anywhere, so I never did anything—that is, until I got up in age. Now, I'm sixty-three and starting to write books. Crazy, isn't it?

I should have started younger. I could have been somewhere with my writing and not worrying from one day to the next. But it's all in the past now, and life goes on as long as you're in it. That's all I know about that.

Well, in Kingston, there was a friend who lived there. He is seventy-three, maybe seventy-four years old now. I talked to him long ago. He was going to join a church one day, but he hasn't yet. You can't make anyone go; it's up to them. But you can talk about Jesus. You'll know right away if they don't really want to hear it. So you slow down, get on to something else. And you can pray for your friend. That's what I've done, and I still will. But he's living somewhere else far away, so I don't know if I'll see him again. I hope someday I will. He can talk about going to church if he wants. That would be great.

CHAPTER 3

About Kingston and the Spot

Well, Kingston is not that big of a place, but you could live there if you wanted to. You could do your shopping there. I've shopped there, I've lived there before, and it's not that bad really. I liked it there. It's a pretty town, and there are still people I know there. I see them once in a while and visit them sometimes.

I like the way Kingston feels, with its pretty plants and flowers along the side of the walkways and not too close to the road. It's wonderful and pretty; I love it. And I like the trails in the woods. Going through the woods is so peaceful. It smells great. I really like the smell of the trees. I spend time in Kingston and love the spot I go to.

CHAPTER 4

In the Winter

In the winter in Kingston, I like the snow. Sometimes, it's not good for driving in, not even with a bike. But I go. And I'm OK as long as I'm careful of the roads, as they can get slippery. I watch out for myself, and I'm fine.

I'm going to do a good job about my spot. I'll get friends and people to come there, and they'll want to. I'll get seats in. That's my plan. We can eat there and drink pop or coffee—but not brew. I don't drink that, and I want that place clean and no drinking booze. It may turn out great. I won't know unless I try. And I do want to try.

Maybe sometime I may want to move back to Kingston. It's close to my spot and still not far from my family. It's just a little longer on the bike to visit; that's all. And I can do that.

Another night has gone, and it's going on twelve o'clock. I'm here at home tonight. Everything seems calm. I don't hear much of anything. And that's good for me; I can write. Back to Kingston—I'll talk more about that. I can write better when it's calm, when nothing's bothering me. I just write. I really like the place in Kingston because it's nice and wonderful, and, to me, it has that pretty look. Like I said before, I have friends there I can still see. And I still go there because my spot is there. I like the trees up on top of that hill.

I picked a title—Pretty Trees on the Hill. I want to see if I can make that into something. I'll ask the owners if I can, and if they say yes, that will be cool. It will take money, I know. And if things go well with this book, maybe it will work. Let's hope.

My home is nice. I painted inside and painted my outside door blue and a nice spot. I have friends here and family close and not too far from the church. I knew I'll be living here for a long time. It is not bad here it is good.

CHAPTER 5

Little Town of Kingston

February 17

I like this little town of Kingston. It's a fantastic place. There's a nice food bank there, where people can go if they're in need. I was down to see my brother Ronnie. We talked about things and about ourselves in the past, and we laughed and had a great time. I feel the Lord is working. I'm a churchgoer, and I believe in Jesus. He is with me.

As I've said, I like the town of Kingston even though it's a small town. It's pretty there, and I like it. I know, I've said that enough times that whoever reads this book will say, "Yes, Larry. We know that by now." Laugh out loud.

I may move back to Kingston sometime. I don't know just yet. I believe Jesus will let me know that part later. I guess there's lots of time for that right now. I like the way the people of Kingston keep things clean and nice. There are paths and benches to sit on in town, more than there are in Greenwood Mall. I ride along these pathways on my bike.

CHAPTER 6

Walking through Kingston

I like walking through Kingston and taking my camera with me. I take photos of this and that and post them on Facebook. People like them, which is good. As for my spot in Kingston, I don't really know what's going to happen there. It could be a big thing. After all, I already got my title up on my spot, and it's a nice title—Pretty Trees on the Hill. It's a great name for my spot. Even the owner agrees; he just loves it. But we'll see what comes out of it. There's a long road that leads to the creek (my name for the river). I go there a lot in the summer. But I go to the Greenwood Mall in Middleton, too, as I have friends to see.

A heart nailed to a tree that says Pretty Trees On The Hill, and anyone can come bring a seat And sit, and it is to my spot i go to i love it there.

CHAPTER 7

Love This Town

I'm here in my bedroom in the town of Kingston and now getting that time to work on my spot. I love this town, and the snow is falling, and that is good. I like walking or riding my bike to the creek. It will be nice again; it will be fun. There's a coffee shop there, which I'll be going to. Then I'll head to my spot, where I'll sit for a bit. I'll find seats so I can sit down. And I'll be walking through Kingston to see if there are friends out, because I'll want to share my spot.

Well, I told my family about my spot. But they won't be in this book much. It's more about my spot I've found. I do like having friends come to it, but if it gets too out of hand, I may lose my spot. Let's hope not—let's hope things will be OK. There's a store to go to, where I can get pop. I drink a lot of pop and coffee.

CHAPTER 8

Town of Love

Thursday, March 26

Well, the town of love is still Kingston—just to let you know what you're still reading. I'll go there soon, see how things are going, and ride around a bit. There are other places I do go to, but I can't wait to see my spot again. I want to clean things up there and make it nice and ride to the creek.

I still see and visit my family, Shirley and Henry, and I'll stop at my brother's. But this virus is going all around the world, and people are dying. It's not good. And it's not over. It's hard to say if we're going to be here—if we'll get sick and die. I can't say for sure, but I wanted to write about it here. It's the biggest thing we've had yet, as far as I can remember. And I hope and pray that they can stop it, and we can live our good lives out. I know we all leave this world one day, but I hope not like this.

There are things I want to do while I'm still here. I'd like to get my first book out. I started this one, but I don't know if it will get out. It will have more pages and maybe photos; that's what I'm hoping anyway. It's Friday, April 10, here. I am again at my desk in the bedroom. It's 8:10 p.m. It's snowing hard here, and we still have to stay home because the virus is still ongoing. People are still carrying it. It is not good at all.

CHAPTER 9

Good, oh, Kingston

Kingston is OK. I like going there. There are still things I want to do there, when this virus is stopped—if it ever is. I go for walks. There are many places to go, and I want to find them. It's Friday, the eighth. The virus is still hanging on. I hope it gets stopped; it's slowing everything down. But I've been in Kingston cleaning my spot and getting it ready. I want to get some seats made or gear up something there and make a garbage bin to put garbage in. That will be cool.

CHAPTER 10

Going to Kingston to Get Things Fixed Up

Well, I've been in Kingston off and on getting things done. When I get what I want done, I can take a break and go there to drink coffee or pop and have lunch too. I will have a bin for garbage by then, which will be great. I'll let the owner know, so he knows what's going on and find out if it's OK for me to do that. It's Sunday May 10, and I was at my spot in Kingston the other day. I got a garbage bin fixed up for the garbage for now; it'll work until I get something better.

It's windy today. I'm home sitting around. I'll go to Kingston again soon, but I don't think I'll be going to my spot today. It's too windy out for riding the bike, so I'll find something to do here at home. Oh, I know. I'll write.

CHAPTER 11

To My Spot

Friday, May 22

I went to my spot a few days ago. I'm getting things cleaned up now. I need to get a rake, but it's looking good. And somehow, I need to get seats here. I need to think of a way. I may find something to make into a seat or seats. Either way, I get to the spot once in a while. I like it there. It's a nice place.

Tuesday, May 26

I'm home here on my front step now. It's cooling down. It's been a good day. I went to my spot in Kingston and cleaned up a bit. Then I rode into town and went to the trailer park, which is down from Kingston a little. It's a nice ride there along a trail. There's not a lot to do right now, but I'll get back to working on my spot again soon.

[the Creek] i go here and it is great you can fish here but i don't, i
sit here on a big rock and enjoy myself it is nice here.

CHAPTER 12

In Kingston to Get My Bench Done

Sunday, June 14

I'm in Kingston to get my bench done. It's built now, and in some time, I'll paint it. But at least now I can sit without hurting my back, which is great. I have the back of the bench built now. So that's good. There's a bit of grass at my spot, and it's all mowed; I got that cut. As for the golf field, the owners mowed that. Now it looks so pretty. The trees here are great. I just love it here. The tower is close and very high. I like that. And people are playing golf up at the top of the spot where I sit. It's nice to watch and not so sunny. It's cool, which is great. I love it when the sky is all blue and pretty on the great sunny days when I'm here. Sometimes, I ride my bike up to the creek (my name for the nearby running river). Plain creek sounds better to me. It's not far from the spot really, but I like riding to the creek, which runs along the path near the spot I go to. It's great.

CHAPTER 13

I Am at My Great, Loving Spot

Sunday, June 21

I'm at my great, loving spot today, writing in my book. It's nice and cool. Looking around me, I see nice-looking, pretty trees. I always love trees, as you can see, and the trails and pathways I walk on are absolutely wonderful. I like walking or riding my bike along the trails. The weather's nice, and the grass is starting to get tall. I'll have to get at that soon with my whipper snipper.

People are playing golf today. I see them walk by, and they see me sitting on my bench. I wave to them. I think they wonder what I'm doing over here. Laugh out loud. I get to talk to some of the golfers if they're close by. I tell them this is my spot and that the village people said it was OK. I say I feel great here. It's a nice place to be.

"Nice," the golfers say.

I say, "Yup," and, "It's cool here." I tell them how I built my own bench to sit on and that I like the golf field.

The guys play on.

The grass is mowed low and nice, and it's green. It's important to keep the grass cut low, so the golfers can see the golf balls and the holes. It's pretty.

My spot has a small hill similar to the one on *Little House on the Prairie*. I call my spot the Pretty Trees on the Hill. If anyone comes here to have a seat, I don't leave my bench there when I leave. It might get taken. So, I left it at a friend's in Kingston.

I'm thinking of bringing my guitar to have a singsong before winter. That will be fun.

CHAPTER 14

At My Spot Watching People Play Golf

At my spot watching people play golf, I'm happy. I finished the bench I built, so I have a great bench. I won't be staying here long. I put a lot of work into the bench. I just wanted to get things done before winter.

The book is mostly about my spot. But I'll talk about other things here—like Kingston. It's a small town, so there's nothing there to go on about too much. But I will find more things to talk about before the book is done.

I'm home now, writing. I'll be going down to Kingston tomorrow I guess. I'll find more things to write about. There are other things I want to look at, and I'll take my camera to see what I can fine. I'll keep writing the book, and that will be cool, I'd say.

No one came in today. I'm all alone. I seem to write best that way. I can write all night, and I have. If something comes up, I have to write it down and keep going—laugh out loud. It's early, 7:00 p.m. But I can't hear anyone out anywhere. Everyone's indoors I guess. That's good anyway. I'm fine here, doing my own thing—and that is writing.

CHAPTER 15

Painting My Bench

Monday, June 22

At the spot in Kingston, I did a little painting on my bench. The color is a pretty blue, and it's a nice-looking bench now. The sun is out again—another hot day. But I'm under the trees, where it's shady and wonderful. It's just great. I do a lot of my writing here. In winter, I'll be at home writing at my desk, but I'm at my spot now. I seem to do well here. I guess the words just come to me when I write.

They are mowing on the golf field. It is getting long. I have to mow my spot soon to get it looking nice again. I'll get it done.

CHAPTER 16

Back to Work

Wednesday, June 24

I worked this morning, and I'm going back to work at 7:00 p.m. for two hours. That's all. I'm at my spot in Kingston for a bit and watching people golf again, sitting on my bench. It's another hot day, but it's cool at my spot—my great place. Another day, I think I'll go out to town in Kingston. I'll find more things to write about. I'll move around a bit, and I'll find more things to do in town.

Another Towler, they are all great, I like them I never climbed
one and don't think so, but they are great

Here in Kingston, Looks like Rain

Tuesday, June 30

Down here in Kingston, it looks like it's going to rain. But I wanted to fix my bench, and people are golfing today. Plus, I haven't cut my grass here at my spot yet; I have to get at it. A helicopter is flying around here today—I don't know why—and flying close. I won't stay long, as it's going to rain. I have to get out of here, or I'll get wet.

Thursday, July 16

I'm back at home here today. It seems I never get to Kingston lately. I've been busy and haven't gotten to it. But I will. I still have things to do there. I want to get it done, so when I get the free time, I'll get there. Now, I have work to do. I'm just waiting for the call. I need to make a little money, so I can get things I need from the stores. Ha! We all need money to get by nowadays. I know I need it.

This is the Rink, i go here when they have something going on, before Christmas they have Hot dog's apple sider and hot chili and i watch the kids skate and the parents and other one's skate man great skaters I see they are having great fun.

[The Duck Pond] i like the duck pond, i go there sometimes, they have benches
to sit on, I like seeing the ducks and kids people feeding them

CHAPTER 18

Talking about Kingston Town

Kingston is a wonderful town. Really it is. There are many places I need to find. I ride all around the place in Kingston and up around the schools. I was glad to take a photo of the school for my book. I called and got the OK. They have nice schools here. As I ride past them, they look big. I see the kids playing outside, and I ride up around the skating rink and watch them skate. It's cool. A lot of them skate well; there are some great skaters here. I used to skate. I still can, but I have no skates. And I'm sixty-three now, so I don't skate much. But I should get skates and try. I know I still can.

My spot is still where I go and rest a bit. I watch the golfers play golf and have fun. They win money and other things. It's a fun game, but I've never played it. Maybe I should. I may like it.

It looks like rain here; it might start soon. I have work to do. I have to wait for another day, when there's no rain. I'll just be in the house, but there's not much to do right now. I hope we work today.

i love going to the Needs Store, i used to when i lived in Kingston, i still do
If i am down there, they all know me and they are great people.

CHAPTER 19

The Post Office in Kingston

I'm here at home writing about Kingston and about my spot. I haven't gotten down to Kingston lately, and it's raining so won't be the day. Well, about Kingston, there's a post office there. It used to be a CIBC bank, which is where I bank, but not now. So I go to Greenwood Mall CIBC branch to do my banking. As for the post office in Kingston, I still go there even though I don't live there now. I go to mail something or get stamps. You can't get stamps in Greenwood Mall anymore, I don't think. I know I used to get them there frequently and mail my stuff right there. But now I go to the Kingston post office.

Man, how things change all the time. But that's fine with me. I go to Kingston a lot anyway—no big deal. You can't stop what changes. You just go with it; that's all you can do, laugh out loud. I can still get my stuff done; that's the main thing.

I'm going to Kingston today. I have to go to the post office anyway. I have to mail something. It was raining last night, but it's not so bad out today—maybe a little windy. But I need to go to Kingston anyhow. I'll be going in a few, and I'll do more writing.

[Bridge] this is the bridge me and a friend come to, we look over it see the water, it gets low water and sometimes it is high and pretty trees around there we like

CHAPTER 20

More about Kingston

Here at home, I'm looking out my window. I see Tom and Patsy next door, and I'm looking at the pretty, tall trees they have over there. The kids—Patsy's grandkids–like playing around them. They have fun, but they're getting pretty much grown up now.

I need to get to Kingston again because soon it'll be winter and cold. I'll bring home the bench I built and save it for next summer. But I'll still go to Kingston. I won't be able to do too much at my spot in the winter.

It's still summer, though. So I'll be able to work at my spot, where I used to live in Kingston. I'll go up and around my spot, along the path that is so sweet and nice. I love it. I'll ride all along it. I'll run into my friends, and I'll talk to them.

"What are you doing?" they may ask.

"Just writing," I'll say. "Give me something to do."

If I'm not writing in Kingston, I write at home, which is where I am now. Time goes by quickly. I lay down a bit, and I fall asleep. I get back up if I feel like writing. I get my book and go at it. It's best to write alone because you know what you're writing. You're thinking word after word, and the pen is just a moving—laugh out loud. I love writing when I'm at it.

[Towler] this is a great photo of the Towler they are high.

CHAPTER 21

Cool and Daylight

August 13

I'm here in Kingston at my very great spot. It's 8:56 in the morning, but it's cool and daylight, so I can write. I'll be going to the Greenwood Mall later, and I might see my friend who lives across from the Greenwood Mall. I'm in Kingston now, and I see people are out playing golf today. It's cool for now, but I think it will turn out to be a hot day. I'm sitting here on my garbage bin, which I placed in the shade. It's cool. I believe next time I'll go out in town; I seem to write about other things—whatever I see around me.

The bears are out and about. They've been spotted around here. They're tired, and they have no food, so they come looking for food the best way they can find it. They have to eat. So whenever you see a bear, just look out. Don't get close and try to get away slowly. Don't run. That will get the bear chasing you. Just be careful.

Well, there's not much to write about where I am right now—just the pretty, tall trees. So, I guess I'll move on.

***

Now I'm down in Kingston again. It looks like something's going on here across from the rink. I believe there will be singing. It's nice here. The grass is all mowed. It looks great. I used to live right up above here. Well, you can't see. I'll have to take pictures next time for this book.

I go to the rink when there are fun things going on there, like just before Christmas. There are summer events, too, with hot dogs and pop and all that stuff. Where there is food there, there is me. No, not really—laugh out loud. I just came to hear them sing.

Now the musicians are getting started. I didn't know anyone would be here today. I'll hear them sing and play guitar. There are musicians singing here often. I just didn't think there'd be a show today. But everything has worked out great. I love it.

CHAPTER 22

Back in Kingston This Morning

Sunday, August 16

I'm back in Kingston this morning. I'd come to get my whipper snipper anyway, so I thought I'd write a bit at my spot. It's 9:27 a.m., and it's daytime. The golfers are out; they always are. I guess it must be a fun game. But I'll move on to another spot for a bit today and write some more, I think.

***

I've moved from my spot, and I'm out by the highway now. You can see Needs from here. I don't go there a lot, because I'm not living in Kingston. But when I lived here, I went to the Needs store almost every day. It's a nice store, and the people who work there know me well. I do like going there. I get pop and that. Lots of cars are going by today, but not many people are walking around. It's getting hot anyway.

Now, I think I'll go home. It is 10:48 in the morning. I'm just writing when I have free time, and I love writing. I think better when I'm out writing—when I write about Kingston. Well, I guess I'll get going; I'll move on to different places in Kingston to see what to write down.

CHAPTER 23

Going to Town

Thursday, August 20

I'm home writing tonight—about Kingston. I wasn't down to Kingston today, so maybe I'll go tomorrow. I feel better writing right in Kingston. The words just come out. But home here, not much is going on.

I do a show now on stream. I have a tree I call Jake, Jake the tree. It's pretty cool. And I sing a bit too to start the show. I call myself Larry the Seller. My viewers all love the show, so it's great.

I keep busy when I'm not writing, but I do want to keep up my writing. I feel I do well with that. I visit my friends and my family too. It's all good.

Sunday, August 23

I am at the Greenwood Mall right now. I was in church, but I came here to the Greenwood Mall. I'll stay for a bit and then go to Kingston and, after that, to my spot. I'll sit there for a while. It's a Sunday and nice day, not too bad out. A bunch of people are here at the Greenwood Mall, and more are coming in. I'm here drinking my coffee.

No one I know is here yet, none of my friends. But I may see some yet. There was one friend here. He doesn't talk a lot, but he's a great friend. He just left, but he lives down in Kingston. I'll be going there in a bit.

[Post Office] i like coming here to mail my stuff, it is nice here.

CHAPTER 24

This Is Sunday

At the Greenwood Mall, I look around to see if I can spot anyone I know. But I haven't yet. This is Sunday, so I don't know; they may come. Well, I'm about to go to Kingston. I'll see what's up down there.

***

So, I'm in Kingston now. It looks like something's going on here today. Cars are coming in. They're pulling up to the place where musicians sing on Thursdays. But this is Sunday, so I'm not sure what's going on yet. There's a playground down here too, outside something like a school—well, I think it's a school. I see kids sometimes playing on the grounds anyway, and it looks like fun. A lot of people are coming in with cars, so something is going on. We'll see.

***

I'm at my spot here in Kingston. It's a nice, sunny Sunday day, and the golfers are out playing the course. It's a little windy and cool. I won't stay here long. I'll go back and see what was going on at the singing spot in Kingston.

I left to come to my spot, because whatever was going on hadn't started yet. But I'll go back and see anyway.

***

I did leave my spot, and now I'm getting close to the goings-on here across from the rink in Kingston. Whatever it is has started, and I believe I hear singing now. I'm still far away, but the song sounds great.

CHAPTER 25

Where I Was Today

Friday, August 28

I came to the Greenwood Mall. I had to pay a few bills. I got it done by 1:40 p.m. I'm going to Kingston from here for a bit. A guy owes me money anyway, so I'll get myself that coffee money—laugh out loud.

A lot of people went to the Greenwood Mall today, and more are coming. That's good. It's good people are getting out. Where I was today—in the Greenwood Mall and in Kingston, a lot of people were out and about. Well, it was a great day to be out.

I like coming to the Greenwood Mall, and I do come here a lot. But my spot in Kingston is where I like to be. That's what *Pretty Trees on the Hill* is all about really. I write about other stuff too, though, stuff that readers may like. Everywhere I go, I end up writing. I do carry whatever notepad I'm currently writing in with me. I love writing books.

I see a happy family—a young lady with kids. The baby boy is looking around and laughing. I watch the cute family. It's very nice to see happy people

I'm drinking pop now. I'm parched. I had to have pop. I can drink pop a lot; that's for sure. I never get enough of it.

I'll be getting home soon. I have things to do at home—some cleaning and washing dishes and pots. I'm having pretty good days getting things done. I ride around on the bike a lot. It's the only way I get around. But that's fine; it keeps me in shape.

***

Sunday, August 30

I went to the Greenwood Mall. I don't think I'll be in Kingston today. But I'll get down to doing things at my spot—see how it is. A lot of people are coming in today. It's a nice place to come. I get things here at the dollar store—things I work with.

While drinking my coffee at the mall and watching people walk around, I was taking the time to write a bit.

Soon, I'll be going home to get things done around the house. I'm always on the go. I was just in church, and I came here to the Greenwood Mall afterward.

***

Well, I'm home now and resting until next time.

Tuesday, September 1

I'm at the Greenwood Mall again. I left early so I can get around and do my thing like I always do—that is, writing. I'm in the back of the Greenwood Mall because it's not open yet. So I'm writing until 10:00 a.m. It's almost there, so not long. And there aren't too many people around yet, they will be people coming.

CHAPTER 26

We All Like the Mall

The Greenwood Mall is open, so I got my coffee. I'm here in N.S. People are coming to the Greenwood Mall now. We all like the Greenwood Mall. It's a great place. I used to work here as a cleaner, but things slowed down on account of the virus. My friends are still working there, though—for how long, I don't know. a lot of people do a lot of shopping here at the Greenwood Mall. I do, at the dollar store, when I have the money on paycheck day.

Well, I was in Kingston at my spot. The golfers are golfing again today, and it's a great day for it. We'll lose these great days because winter's going to hit. We all know that. And I won't be in Kingston as much. It'll be too cold.

I see the great trees here. I like them—these trees at my pretty spot.

[BAND STAND] this is the place they come and sing, great place i use to bring my laptop here And get on Wi-Fi and i would hear them play and sing

CHAPTER 27

At the So-Called Mall We All Like

Thursday, September 3

Well, I'm at the so-called Greenwood Mall we all like. I'm drinking my coffee and looking around to see who I know and do a little shopping. I need to get a few things and then go home.

To get around, I ride my bike. I ride to Kingston because the book is about Kingston, and I write things about it, like what the town looks like. But I write other stuff, too, like the Greenwood Mall and other places here that people may like.

It's getting busy here. People are coming in. They like them all a lot too. But you can't hang around long, on account of the virus. You drink your coffee and move on. That's how it is—until it gets stopped if it ever does. I hope so.

I don't have my camera with me today. But next time, I'll bring it to take more pictures for the book. I'll get moving on. I've finished my coffee, so I'll go to the cheap stores, like the dollar store—laugh out loud.

Soon, I'm in Kingston up where the school is. It's a nice big school, as it's now right across from me. I'll take a picture of it for this book. I go past it a lot. And I'm glad about today—getting around, writing, and taking photo shoots. I'll be going to my spot as soon as I leave this place.

Saturday, September 5

I go everywhere here in Kingston. There are surely some pretty trees around here. But it's getting to be winter. It's getting cold now, but it's nice and sunny today.

I'm at my spot now to see how things are. Everything is looking good. I'm just getting things put away for winter. I'll bring them back in the summer. I got my bench home now. I can't leave that here all winter. I still have my garbage bin here at my spot. I'll leave that. I can sit on its cover, like I'm doing now, and do whatever I do. And that is writing.

I like drinking pop or eating chips. That will be my lunch for a while.

I just wanted my bench home where it's safe. I'll bring it back in the summertime. There are still things to do here. I hope to get it all done.

CHAPTER 28

Taking Photos

Sunday, September 6

I just left church. The service was over, and now I'm down in Kingston. I'm going out in town to take some photos. I think I'll get moving on. I'll get out around town and see what I can see and all that. It's a nice day again.

I'm sitting at my spot. People are playing golf here—as they do every day. But it's a good game, I'd say. Anyway, I'm leaving my spot now. I was in town. I took pictures of the post office. I got a great photo of it. I hope you'll see it in this book.

CHAPTER 29

Home at My Place

Saturday, September 12

I'm at my place. It's Saturday and nice out. I haven't gotten to Kingston yet but will tomorrow, I guess, to see my spot. I don't go there much now. I keep busy, but I'm not done there yet. Still, my bench is made, and I have it home now. I don't want it out all winter. But I go to my spot. When I go, I sit on the box cover I still have there—if it's still there. I will see, laugh out loud. There's nothing left that someone could take. I took my saw and bench home. I'll take my bench back to my spot next year. For now, I'll find things to sit on. It's getting a bit cold now to go to my spot anyway. But I'll take winter pictures.

CHAPTER 30

Sit Here at My Spot in Kingston

Sunday, September 13

I'm sitting here at my spot in Kingston. I just got out of church. So, I've come here to Kingston to do some writing. There are people golfing, like always. But it's fun to them, and that's great; it gives them something to do, and they win money and other things, which is good.

It's a great day anyway. The sun is out, still being summer. But I just come here when I can. I took my bench home for the winter. I still have my garbage box here. That will stay. It gives me something to sit on. I just sit on the cover until winter hits. It will be covered with snow then. But that will be fine. It won't hurt it much; it's just an old, old wooden box. It's not that good anyway. So, I can use that to sit on for now, when there are still fine days. Come wintertime, I won't be here as much. The snow will be too deep and all that.

I may go into town before I head home. I'll get some more pictures taken. I'll leave my spot soon and ride around to the spots where I'll take pictures.

***

I left my spot, and I'm out in town now. It looks busy here in town, with all the cars going by and people getting their outdoor cleaning done before the snow. It's good that they're getting their things done.

CHAPTER 31

The Bandstand

This is a nice, great place to come—this place where musicians come to play guitar and sing. I come to hear them sing. Great singers play and sing here. A lot of people come and bring their lawn chairs. They sit and clap their hands, cheering on each person who sings. It's really fun, and anyone who wants to can come and hear them sing. The shows are great fun, and we all have a wonderful time. I should include a photo of a show on one of the pages.

CHAPTER 32

Duck Pond in Kingston

Monday, September 14

I'm here at the duck pond in Kingston, but I'm thinking of slowing down. The time is 10:50 a.m. There are some nice, pretty ducks here. People feed them, putting out bread and duck seed that they eat; they're good to the ducks. This is a nice place to come to watch the ducks. They come right up to the banks, and they're pretty to watch.

I guess I'll get moving on down to town and see what's going on.

***

I went into town, and now I'm home. It's now 1:27 p.m.

***

Time is ticking. It's 7:20 p.m., and I'm lying down on the couch, thinking and wanting to write again. The words just come out at me, and it's not a bad night. It's cool; I'm fine. And I heard it'll be nice tomorrow, so I hope I'll have work. I'm just here looking at my four walls and thinking.

When people come in, they see I have a lot of pictures up. I do. The people who know me know some of the people who are in the photos, some taken years ago. I've saved them, and I hang a lot of pictures up.

I'll be going to Kingston again when I get the chance. I want to do a lot more in Kingston because much of *Pretty Trees on the Hill* is about Kingston. There's not too much to write tonight—at least not right now. But if I think of something, I'll be writing.

CHAPTER 33

What a Rainy Day

I'm at the Greenwood Mall because I need to get a few things, and man, what a rainy day. A hurricane-level storm was predicted, but it wasn't as bad as we'd thought it would be. It's just raining now, but the rain should be done by night. I never got to Kingston today; it's too wet to ride the bike there. Here at the Greenwood Mall, people are coming and going. They're busy getting things at the Greenwood Mall, or they come for coffee and have their breakfast. That's good. People want to get out.

There are more pictures I want to take in Kingston for my book, so I'll do that when I get the chance to get down there. Kingston is small but nice. I like it there. I may live there again. I'd be away from the church again. I'd still get there, but in *God's* time.

I don't want to keep moving around. So, I'll stay where I'm at until I feel I need to move on. I plan to stay here, but I do want something better than a trailer. I hope that happens for me. But I'm closer to family here really. I don't want to move too far away, but Kingston isn't far. And I would like to have a better place. I have no car. I just ride the bike. If I were in Kingston I could use the bike, and I could still visit family and get to church. But right now, I won't worry about that.

[guitar] my guitar i play and sing, i make up my own songs, i
have lots I wrote Down people like my singing

53

CHAPTER 34

Not a Bad Night

It's OK here—not a bad night. I see out my window, and the weather looks good. I'm home doing some writing. Soon, I have to do house cleaning. Things add up when you're busy doing something; it doesn't take long.

I had nothing to do, so I thought I would write some. Allen, Ronnie's son, messaged me and wanted me to come out. So I went, and we played two or three games of pool, which is a fun game. I got a can of pop—they gave me one—so I'm drinking that. It was raining. It stopped, but it might rain some more.

The forecast said it's going to rain. But that's fine. I'll stay in and write. I like to write; it's something I'm good at. I don't have the TV on much now.

I got myself back into writing, but I do still visit just the same. If I'm not visiting, my people wonder why I'm staying home. But I don't want to give it out that I'm home writing. They would try and talk me out of it. They know it's costly when you start writing books. They think I'll spend all my money and get nowhere. But I hope that doesn't happen—that this will work out for me, and I'll make money off my books. But anyway, I still want to try.

It's early yet—only 7:05 p.m., so I have a little time yet to write. There's not too much going on now. I'm here at home, looking around and out my windows—not a soul around. I hear cars going by, and that's about all I hear.

Well, I guess I'll stop for now.

[The school] the school is a big long school, it looks great and lots of play ground For the kids and bigger ones to that come out to the play grounds it is pretty there.

CHAPTER 35

I Am at My Spot

I'm here in Kingston. I got to my spot, and it's not a bad day. It's pretty good, actually. The golfers were out playing golf at any rate, and the sun was out. It was a little windy, but not much. Well, I guess the grass mowing is done for the year. It's coming in winter, so I won't mow here at the spot, I don't think, until next year. The grass is growing some, but that's OK. I had to bring the whipper snipper down all the time on the bike. If things go well next year, I'll be here mowing. It's 11:06 a.m., and I won't stay long today.

Well, I guess I'll take off for now; it is 11:11 a.m.

The trails i take out back of my place at the trailer park and in the
woods this trail i can go to my brothers this way it is cool

CHAPTER 36

The Day Seems OK

Saturday, October 3

There wasn't much to do. So I came to the Greenwood Mall this morning. The time is 10:24 a.m. I had to get my GST anyway, and I owe my landlord money. So, I have to do that. I'll give him some on the bill as a hold until I get paid. And I have to get to Kingston and take more pictures. There are still a lot of places I want to photograph for this book. Right now, I'm drinking coffee here at the Greenwood Mall just to kill time. It gives me something to do.

I want to get the book done. That would be nice. I buy notebooks to write in; I bought one a few minutes ago. And I keep on writing.

Today seems OK. The forecast says there'll be some sun. But it's early in the morning—well it's 10:39 a.m.—so the day is just getting started. It may get better through the day. I do get up early, and I pray to get the day going. Then I start getting out to do what I do. And that's writing. I hope my books are interesting for readers to read.

More people are coming into the Greenwood Mall today. They got out this morning, and some got here as soon as it opened up, same as me. I'm waiting. I got here this morning when it was opening (at 10:00 a.m.), and now it's 10:24. That's early on a Saturday.

The Greenwood Mall now opens throughout the week at 10:00 a.m.—which is because of the virus. It used to open at 7:00 a.m.

Well, I had my coffee, and it's almost gone. When the coffee is gone, I'm gone for a bit. I have to leave anyway when I'm done drinking the coffee. Because of the virus, you can't really hang around like you could before. I would have to buy another coffee if I came back to the table in order to keep sitting here.

Some more trails where i live this trail goes out to the highway.

CHAPTER 37

I Got to Kingston

Sunday, October 4

I got to Kingston. I'm here now. It's a little windy, but it's not a bad day. It's actually pretty good out, and I will go out and about around town here after a bit. I like getting out all I can while there are good days. It will get cold soon, as it's fall now.

People are picking apples, which is good. You can make good money doing that. My brother does. He likes picking apples and gets hours for his E1.

Well, I guess that's enough to stay at my spot here. I guess I'll leave for now. It's 1:24 p.m. I went to the mall again after church, but it was the same old thing—not a lot was going on there. But the day wasn't too bad. People came and drank coffee and ate, laugh out loud. They had their dinner here I guess. I wasn't here long.

CHAPTER 38

Not Much to Do at Home

Mon, October 5

Well, there wasn't much to do at home, so I was at the Greenwood Mall. It was a little cold this morning. I went home and then came back to the Mall again by bus.

Sunday, November 14, 2021

I got to the Mall just now. I got a pop, and I'm just sitting here. A lot of people are here. I came to get pens and stuff to write with. I'll be going soon. I'm just trying my new pen. It works well, and it's a great day. After the wind we had last night, today turned out OK.

***

I'm home now writing. It's late 12:11 a.m. But soon, I'll go to bed. I'll write more later when I get up. I need to sleep now, so I'll get back to writing more after that.

Photo of the turn on the right is where the spot is, you can hardly
see the bike but it is there if you look real good.

CHAPTER 39

I Find It Nice Here at Home

I'm here at home tonight. The people next door still have their lights on. But it's only 9:05 p.m. And I find it nice here tonight. But it'll be cold tomorrow, I bet. I won't be going anywhere too far. I'll just stay home and write. I have nothing better to do. It'll give me more time to think about what to write down.

My friend James comes here a lot, and we go for coffee. We go to my brother Ronnie's, and we play pool, trying to win a few games. It's fun playing pool. I won some. I like it. And we play the guitar and sing a little. We like doing that.

Plus, I make videos with me singing. My friends say I do a great job singing. I make up my own songs—I talk a lot about Kingston. No, not really. There are other things I talk about—like how we have our good times. I sing about how things go with our friends and having fun like that is wonderful. But anyway, things are good.

CHAPTER 40

Here with My Radio On

I have fun at home with the radio on. I hear songs I like, which is great, and I hear the news. I don't know what I'll be doing tomorrow. Not much. I know I need a job. I need to find one somewhere. I like to get work and make some money. I know I want to take more photos when I get around to it. And I'd like to get to the store to restock on pop. I ran out, and I need my pop. So maybe tomorrow, if it doesn't rain, I'll go out. But they're calling for it, so I don't know yet. I'll have to wait and see, I guess. I hope I pass the test and get my driver's license. The test is coming up soon. I do practice driving some, but I need to do a lot more practicing if I want to pass. But anyway, so much for that.

The Sign, it is the sign when you first walk in, to get to my spot not far up.

CHAPTER 41

Another Day

Tuesday, November 23

It's another day, and I'm here at home. It's rainy and wet, and I never got to Kingston today—or anywhere, for that matter. But I'll get down there. For now, I'm just home, taking it easy, writing a bit. I do want to get to my spot when the weather is good to take some more pictures. I want to do that and get that done. I'm just writing about things up my way near home for now, but nothing much is going on. It's just too wet out; I don't want to ride my bike today. So, I'll wait for a good day for it to go to Kingston.

It may start clearing up. I think the rain has stopped. I'm looking out my window, and it doesn't look like it's raining.

Anyway, my friend and I played guitar and sang last night. I didn't get to bed until one o'clock in the morning, so I'm a little tired today. But I can write. My friend isn't back yet. But he will be. And I may go out a bit.

I'll stop for now, though, until I find more things to write about.

***

I fell asleep. I just got up. Well, I've been on the computer a bit. But then I got back to writing. I want to go out. I want to get more pictures taken for the book. I'll see. It's almost three o'clock now

***

I took more photos—three of them—and now it's four o'clock in the afternoon. And it's cold. I'm doing more writing. I'm almost done with this chapter. I'm in now, where it's warm. I'll stay in, I guess. I have things to do in my home anyway. So I'll close up on this chapter.

[The Super Store] i like the super store it is a nice store to go too, i get good deals here on Meat and other stuff, i sometimes do my shopping here.

CHAPTER 42

Things Are Going Well

I'm sitting here writing tonight. My friend went home. He may be back. It's late now—12:30 at night—so he may stay home. I can't see him coming back now, but it's hard to say. I have nothing to do right now, so I thought I would write a few pages. I hope tomorrow I may get out a bit. I'd like to get around and take more pictures again. There are a few more things down in Kingston I'd like to get photos of.

I didn't forget Kingston. I like it down there, so I'll go visit. I want to get to my spot. There's not much to do there now, and it's getting cold. Still, I'll go there to see how things are looking. I'll ride around the town of Kingston a bit and see what pictures I can still take.

I ask about the photos I take. I called the stores down in Kingston, and I can take the pictures of the super store and the post office and Needs store and of the school and the rink. I explained it was all for *Pretty Trees on the Hill*, and they wished me good luck. So, I hope it all happens, and they will all get a book.

My radio's on, and the station's playing some good songs. I play around and pick on my guitar and sing a bit to pass the time away. I don't get bored. I keep busy. And I get a writing session in. So everything is good. Things are going well.

I must get ready for bed—see what tomorrow brings.

more trails this trail don't go to my brothers it goes the other way great walking love it it is wonderful

CHAPTER 43

Snowing This Morning

Wednesday, November 24

I just got up a few minutes ago, and it was snowing this morning. It's 8:37 a.m. Wow, the ground is getting white. Well, it's been getting to be that time. I need to dig our shovels out and get them ready. It didn't seem that long ago that we had summer. Time goes by fast. Before we know it, a new season is here.

Well, winter will come and go just as quickly—it, too, will be gone just like that. But a lot of people don't like winter. It's hard for driving, and people don't have the time to do the shoveling, but they do it anyway; they have to if they want to get out, so they can get to work.

I got cleaned up and shaved, and then I had the feeling it was time to start getting into some writing. So, that's what I'm doing now. I want to get it done before my friend arrives. I know he's coming, and he'll be showing up soon. I want to get as much writing in as I can. Plus, I have to type it all up so I can send the manuscript when I'm done.

Writing a book is a lot of work. It takes time; when someone comes, you have to put your work down. You can't write when someone's here. I can't anyway. You can't think. Besides, they would ask questions. "What are you doing? What are you writing about?" That would mess you up. So, I wait until visitors are gone to write. Or if a friend comes, and we go out, I wait until I get back and I'm alone again. That's just the way it goes.

I'm sitting here on my couch thinking about what to write about. Sometimes, you get lost in thinking and have to wait a day or so to have more thoughts about what to write about. You do get lost in your writing and have to stop a bit—until you have more to write. But I do OK, and I'm doing fine.

Wow, it's snowing pretty good here still; it hasn't stopped. I do like snow. I like walking in it. But if I had a car, I may not like it as much—laugh out loud. But anyway, it's all good.

More nice trails this trail goes out to the trailer park i take it sometimes

CHAPTER 44

At My Brother's

Wednesday, November 24

It's 8:15 p.m. My friend and I were at my brother's earlier tonight. I just got back a few minutes ago and got settled in to start writing. We played pool at my brother's. We had a great time with the fire going. He has a wood stove. I like being around a wood stove. You can't beat that. It's nice and cozy and warm. It's really great. I love it. We all had fun; it was wonderful.

I hope it's not too bad out tomorrow. I'd like to take a few more pictures, and that will be enough. I'd like to get to Kingston. But if not, I do have a lot of pictures I've already taken down in Kingston, and that's good. For now, I'm just sitting here writing along as I'm thinking. It's not really that cold tonight, and things are going well as far as I can see. It snowed earlier, but not enough to stay. It's not even snowing now. We know we're going to get it, though, because winter is coming. It will soon be December, and it'll be cold then.

I'm going to put up Christmas things soon. I'll get things all ready and pretty. That'll be great. Christmas isn't the same these days, but I'll still put stuff up.

Well, I guess that's enough for this page.

I go up this way i keep to the left and turn left when i get to the end
and walk a ways it goes far but great.

CHAPTER 45

A Cold Morning Out

I was out for a bit, and, man, it was a cold morning. I was out taking pictures and came back. I hope it warms up. I'll go out again, but I'll have to wait a while and see; it's cold right now. I'll write. It's too cold to go to Kingston, but I'll see if I can get there. I'm not sure yet.

I'm sitting here now at 12:15 p.m., and nothing is going on. My friend isn't here, but he'll be around. It's raining a little, and I'm still home and have nothing to do right now. So I can write some and work on getting this book done. When my friend comes, we can go out for coffee.

My friend James comes here a lot. And sometimes we go to the dollar store. I do anyway—to get my notebook to write in and good pens to write with. You need good pens to write, and the pens I have now seem to write great. So I'll buy more of them. I think I'll get some work done around my home and then get to writing.

***

I'm back. It took me about twenty minutes or more. But I got things looking better. That's great in case someone comes; it won't look so bad. Well, it wasn't that bad, but I wanted to get it done.

I'm thinking of taking a ride and getting some pop. Or maybe I'll wait until my friend comes and then get a pop. I don't know what to do now. Maybe I'll rest a bit

***

I rested some, and I'm back at this again. It's getting cold now. I was out, and I haven't gotten my pop yet—laugh out loud. No one was out much today. Maybe it's too cold. I'll be writing more on the next page.

So many trails to take we play up here with skidoos it is fun
in the winter time we go all through the trails.

CHAPTER 46

I'd Like to Get to My Spot in Kingston Again

If I can get to my spot in Kingston, that will be great. I'd like to get there again before the snow comes. There's nothing to do there. But I could sit there a bit and ride around. I might take a few more pictures with my camera if I get to Kingston; we'll see. My friend never came in tonight. He might yet, I suppose. But it's now 8:15 p.m., so I'm not sure if he will.

I need to go to the bank tomorrow morning and get my bills paid and get that all done. Then I'll be good for another month. So I'll be busy tomorrow for a while. I'll try to get more writing done if I can—if I get the chance to get at it. Or tomorrow night, I may write some. If so, that will be great.

I'd like to hear from people who get the chance to read my book. Please email me at seliglarry1@gmail.com. I would like that very much. that will get me to write more books.

There's really nothing going on tonight. I watched a movie. That's about it. But it was a pretty good movie. Then I started writing before I went to bed. I'll be getting up and getting going early. The bank opens at 10:00 a.m., so I'll leave at about 9:00 a.m. and stay there until 10:00, so I can get into the bank.

***

I went to help a friend. He had no smokes. He had the money, but I went and got the smokes. He paid me back when I got to his place. Now, I just got back to writing again. It's getting late, so I won't write too much more. I'll write tomorrow, when I get back from paying bills. I'll be back at it.

This is where i walk out to home it is cool.

CHAPTER 47

Got My Things Done at the Mall

Friday, November 26

I was out this morning, and I got my things done at the Greenwood Mall—took care of my bills and all that stuff. Now, I'm home taking time to write some. I got good pens today, or I think they're good. I'm writing with one now; it seems good so far.

Anyway, I haven't gotten to Kingston yet. I don't know if I'll get there. It's rainy and wet. We'll see. Later on, I might get to Kingston.

***

I'm back home now. My friend and I got back from my brother's place. We were there for a while. Now, I'm doing some writing. I got all of my things done today, and I'm glad that's taken care of now until next month. My landlord's coming tonight to get the rent money, and that will be done. Then everything will be good.

It's a rainy night tonight, and there'll be rain tomorrow, I believe. I won't get out tomorrow if it's raining. I'll stay in and write—laugh out loud. I'll be doing something, and I do want to get *Pretty Trees on the Hill* done. But I can't hurry writing. That's when things get messed up in your writing. At any rate, I'll fix it before it gets sent in. But I'm doing well, I guess.

Same as always, nothing much is going on tonight. I'll soon be done with this page. I'll write tomorrow and see what I come up with to write about.

CHAPTER 48

How Was the Night?

I went to bed and got up, feeling the urge to write. It was 11:20 p.m. And how was the night? Well, the night seems OK. It's just that I didn't get a good sleep. I got some sleep in, but I couldn't get back to sleep again. So, I jumped out of bed and got into writing. As for the night, well, it seems like a still night to me. Nothing's going on here. I say it's the best night to do some writing. No one's bothering me or stopping me from doing what I'm doing, so it's good that way. No one's around tonight. I still hear cars going by.

Now, I see that the back tire on my bike is going flat. I need to fix that soon—maybe tomorrow. Or I won't get anywhere; that's for sure. I still want to ride. I will get the bike fixed.

There are more pictures I want to take in Kingston. I hope I'll get the chance to take them. This book is almost done. But I still want a few more pictures in it. Anyway, I'll see about getting them taken. Sometimes, I don't get the chance because my friend comes. He comes in the mornings, and we go out for hours. By the time I get back, it's getting late, and I don't have much time to write. I do get a few pages done, though. Every page helps out.

Like I said, it won't be long before the manuscript will be done, and I'll get it sent out to get published. I want that done. Then I'll be cooking. I'll get the book out for readers to buy—which will be wonderful. I'll start getting money after getting some books sold. Then I'll have money for the next book. I really hope this all works out, and I'll reach my dream.

CHAPTER 49

Out Walking Around

Saturday, November 27

It's been raining some today. I was out walking around and taking more pictures up around my place and the trailer park. I went through the trails and up around the sandpit, which was where I took the pictures. Now, I'm home. It's a wet Saturday. Maybe, I'll go down to Ronnie's tonight. He has his classic songs on, which is fun; there are some great songs. Ronnie, my brother; my friend James; and I will go down. We'll have great times and play pool again. And we'll play guitar and sing and have lots of fun.

I haven't been talking too much about Kingston now. Well, I'm at home and not down in Kingston. I need to be in Kingston in order to write about it. But it's not all about Kingston. I have written about Kingston a lot and about my spot. So, there's not too much to say about those topics.

Since I'm home, I'll write about things up my way. And that's cool. Looking out my window, I see that no one has arrived yet. So, I'm just sitting here. It is in the afternoon.

I haven't been going over to my brother David's much. I keep busy at home, writing and typing. That's what I'll do now. Well, I'm going to end this chapter and move on to the next one.

CHAPTER 50

It's Night Now

Still Saturday, November 27

It's nighttime now. My friend James did come, and we did go to my brother Ronnie's. James and I played a few games of pool. I won a few, so that was great, and we stayed for a while. Then he wanted to get home. It had been snowing but had stopped, so he thought he'd better get going. He'll be back in the morning.

I'm home now, and it's 8:10 p.m. I thought about writing some more—just in another chapter. I don't know what I'll be doing tomorrow—I'll see when I get up—or what the day will be like.

I need to get my bike fixed. I'll take the back wheel off; it has to come off anyway, so I'll get that done. Around my home tonight, I got my dishes washed and took care of a few things. Then I got back into writing.

We'll be going to my brother's again. We always get our coffee, and on a Sunday, we just go talk and chat. It'll be Sunday tomorrow, so maybe we'll play some pool. I'll soon find out anyway. There will be hockey on the radio. I don't care much for it, but other people do. It's a great game to them, and that's wonderful. I'm just not in it. It's fun for others, though, and that's just fine.

Well, this is as far as I'm going with *Pretty Trees on the Hill*. This will be the last chapter I write—until I see about writing another book. I hope you all enjoy the book. Whoever buys one, please let me know.

Written by Larry Selig the final editing

Printed in the United States
by Baker & Taylor Publisher Services